Dear
Dan, Amy,
Imogene, Mirabel
And Jarvis, this year And
I hope continue to
all the ones ahead
make great memories.
Love
Auntie
Glenda
2017

These Christmas Memories Belong to

_____

Ellie Claire® Gift & Paper Corp.
Brentwood, TN 37027
EllieClaire.com
A Worthy Publishing Company

Oh, What Joy!
Our Happy Christmastime Memory Book
© 2013 Ellie Claire Gift & Paper Corp.

ISBN 978-1-60936-848-7

Stock or custom editions of Ellie Claire titles may be purchased in bulk for educational, business, ministry, fundraising, or sales promotional use. For information, please email info @EllieClaire.com.

Art by Heather Solum
Compiled by Jill Olson
Typesetting by Scott Williams | Richmond & Williams

Printed in China

1 2 3 4 5 6 7 8 9 – 18 17 16 15 14 13

christmas celebration

Year _____

Thank you, God, for the joy
of snowy days and nights,
and for the chance
to be a child again.

CHRISTOPHER DE VINCK

Special Guests

_____
_____
_____
_____
_____
_____
_____
_____

Memorable Gatherings

_____
_____
_____
_____
_____
_____
_____
_____

LET IT SNOW!

The star...went ahead of them until it stopped over the place where the child was.
When they saw the star, they were overjoyed. Matthew 2:9-10 NIV

Christmas Eve Celebration

_____
_____
_____
_____
_____
_____
_____
_____

Christmas Day Celebration

_____
_____
_____
_____
_____
_____
_____
_____
_____
_____
_____

christmas Dinner

_____
_____
_____
_____
_____
_____
_____

christmas Traditions Observed

_____
_____
_____
_____
_____
_____
_____
_____

Thoughtful Gestures & Cherished Gifts

_____

_____

_____

_____

_____

_____

_____

_____

_____

_____

_____

_____

_____

_____

_____

_____

_____

At this special time of year: follow the children. Hear the joy in their laughter. See the love in their eyes. Feel the hope in their touch.

christmas Greeting Sent

[Adhere
Christmas card or
newsletter here]

Holiday Photo

[Adhere Photo]

Come, everyone! Clap your hands! Shout to God with joyful praise! Psalm 47:1 NLT

Special Events

Forth to the wood did merry men go, to gather in the mistletoe. Sir Walter Scott

The Best, Funniest, Most Challenging, Touching, Embarrassing, or Amazing Memories of this Christmas

_____
_____
_____
_____
_____
_____
_____
_____
_____
_____
_____
_____
_____
_____
_____
_____

Reflections from the Season

_____
_____
_____
_____
_____
_____
_____
_____
_____
_____
_____
_____
_____
_____
_____
_____
_____
_____
_____
_____

It's the season to be jolly because,
more than at any other time,
we think of Jesus.

MAX LUCADO

christmas celebration

Year _____

 Reflect. Be thankful. Be joyful and at peace. Share the blessings of the season.

Special Guests

_____
_____
_____
_____
_____
_____
_____

Memorable Gatherings

_____
_____
_____
_____
_____
_____

LET IT SNOW!

For a child has been born—for us! the gift of a son—for us! ISAIAH 9:6 MSG

christmas Eve Celebration

_____

_____

_____

_____

_____

_____

_____

_____

_____

christmas Day Celebration

_____

_____

_____

_____

_____

_____

_____

_____

_____

_____

christmas Dinner

_____
_____
_____
_____
_____
_____
_____

christmas Traditions Observed

_____
_____
_____
_____
_____
_____
_____
_____

Thoughtful Gestures & Cherished Gifts

_____

_____

_____

_____

_____

_____

_____

_____

_____

_____

_____

_____

_____

_____

_____

God gives gifts and I give thanks and I unwrap the gift given: joy.   ANN VOSKAMP

christmas Greeting Sent

[Adhere
Christmas card or
newsletter here]

Holiday Photo

[Adhere Photo]

Snowflakes are one of nature's most fragile things, but just look
what they can do when they stick together. VESTA M. KELLY

Special Events

_____

_____

_____

_____

_____

_____

_____

_____

_____

_____

_____

_____

_____

_____

By the extraordinary star, the very heavens indicated His coming. BILLY GRAHAM

The Best, Funniest, Most challenging, Touching, Embarrassing, or Amazing Memories of this christmas

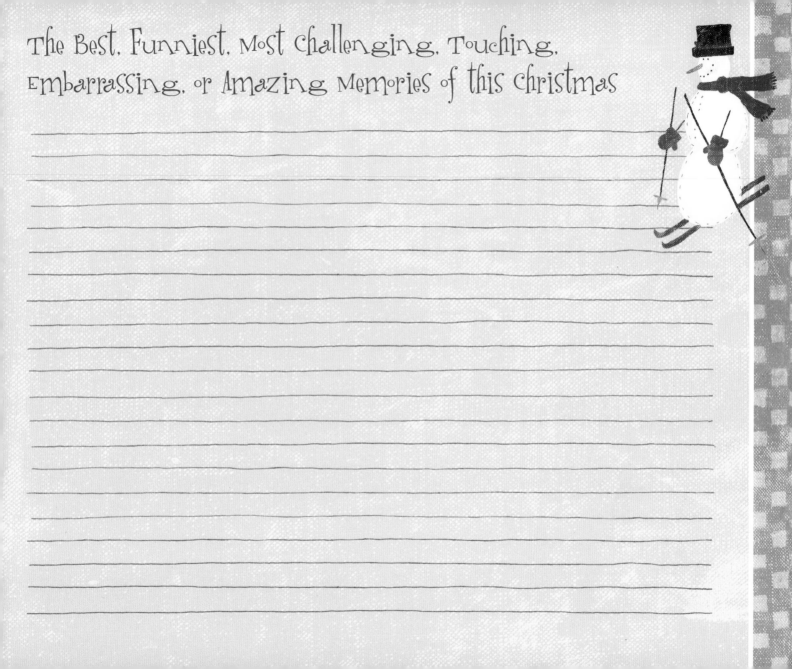

Reflections from the season

_____

_____

_____

_____

_____

_____

_____

_____

_____

_____

_____

_____

_____

_____

_____

_____

_____

_____

Angels we have heard on high
Sweetly singing o'er the plain,
And the mountains in reply
Echoing the joyous strain.

christmas celebration

Year _____

The coming of Jesus at Bethlehem brought joy
to the world and to every human heart. May
His coming this Christmas bring to each one of
us that peace and joy that He desires to give.

MOTHER TERESA

Special Guests

_____

_____

_____

_____

_____

_____

Memorable Gatherings

_____

_____

_____

_____

_____

_____

_____

LET IT SNOW!

Glory to God in the highest heaven, and on earth
peace to those on whom his favor rests.   LUKE 2:14 NIV

Christmas Eve Celebration

_____
_____
_____
_____
_____
_____
_____

Christmas Day Celebration

_____
_____
_____
_____
_____
_____
_____
_____
_____
_____

christmas Dinner

_____
_____
_____
_____
_____
_____

christmas Traditions Observed

_____
_____
_____
_____
_____
_____
_____

Thoughtful Gestures & Cherished Gifts

It is good to be children sometimes, and never better than at Christmas,
when its mighty Founder was a child Himself. CHARLES DICKENS

christmas Greeting Sent

[Adhere
Christmas card or
newsletter here]

Holiday Photo

[Adhere Photo]

Let all that I am praise the Lord; may I never forget the
good things he does for me. PSALM 103:2 NLT

Special Events

_____

_____

_____

_____

_____

_____

_____

_____

_____

_____

_____

_____

_____

_____

_____

_____

Let His joy come to our weary world through us.   GERALD KENNEDY

The Best, Funniest, Most challenging, Touching, Embarrassing, or Amazing Memories of this christmas

_____

_____

_____

_____

_____

_____

_____

_____

_____

_____

_____

_____

_____

_____

_____

_____

_____

Reflections from the season

_____

_____

_____

_____

_____

_____

_____

_____

_____

_____

_____

_____

_____

_____

_____

_____

_____

_____

_____

_____

My heart is content with just knowing
The treasures of life's little things;
The thrill of a child when it's snowing…
Fulfillment that true friendship brings;

JUNE MASTERS BACHER

christmas celebration

Year _____

The joy of brightening other lives…
and supplanting empty hearts and
lives with generous gifts becomes
for us the magic of Christmas.

W. C. JONES

Special Guests

_____

_____

_____

_____

_____

_____

_____

_____

_____

Memorable Gatherings

_____

_____

_____

_____

_____

_____

_____

_____

LET IT SNOW!

She gave birth to her firstborn, a son. She wrapped him in cloths and placed him in a manger, because there was no guest room available for them. Luke 2:7 NIV

christmas Eve Celebration

_____
_____
_____
_____
_____
_____
_____
_____

christmas Day Celebration

_____
_____
_____
_____
_____
_____
_____
_____
_____
_____

Christmas Dinner

_____
_____
_____
_____
_____
_____
_____

Christmas Traditions Observed

_____
_____
_____
_____
_____
_____
_____

Thoughtful Gestures & Cherished Gifts

_____

_____

_____

_____

_____

_____

_____

_____

_____

_____

_____

_____

_____

_____

Then come the wild weather, come sleet or snow,
We will stand by each other, however it blow. SIMON DACH

christmas Greeting sent

[
Adhere
Christmas card or
newsletter here
]

Holiday Photo

[Adhere Photo]

Oh, how my soul praises the Lord.
How my spirit rejoices in God my Savior! LUKE 1:46–47 NLT

Special Events

_____

_____

_____

_____

_____

_____

_____

_____

_____

_____

_____

_____

_____

_____

_____

_____

Christmas is the day that holds all time together. ALEXANDER SMITH

The Best, Funniest, Most challenging, Touching, Embarrassing, or Amazing Memories of this christmas

_____
_____
_____
_____
_____
_____
_____
_____
_____
_____
_____
_____
_____
_____
_____
_____
_____

Reflections from the season

How silently,
How silently the wondrous gift is given.
So God imparts to human hearts
The wonders of His heaven.

PHILLIPS BROOKS

christmas celebration

Year _____

Joyful all ye nations, rise,
Join the triumph of the skies;
With th' angelic host proclaim,
"Christ is born in Bethlehem!"

Special Guests

_____

_____

_____

_____

_____

_____

Memorable Gatherings

_____

_____

_____

_____

_____

_____

LET IT SNOW!

Silent, and soft, and slow,
Descends the snow.   HENRY WADSWORTH LONGFELLOW

christmas Eve Celebration

_____

_____

_____

_____

_____

_____

_____

_____

christmas Day celebration

_____

_____

_____

_____

_____

_____

_____

_____

_____

Christmas Dinner

_____
_____
_____
_____
_____
_____
_____
_____

Christmas Traditions Observed

_____
_____
_____
_____
_____
_____
_____

Thoughtful Gestures & Cherished Gifts

_____

_____

_____

_____

_____

_____

_____

_____

_____

_____

_____

_____

_____

_____

_____

_____

_____

_____

Christmas in lands of the fir-tree and pine, Christmas in lands of the palm-tree and vine,
Christmas where snow peaks stand solemn and white....Everywhere, everywhere, Christmas tonight! PHILLIPS BROOKS

christmas Greeting sent

[Adhere
Christmas card or
newsletter here]

Holiday Photo

[Adhere Photo]

Make my joy complete by being like-minded, having the same love, being one in spirit and of one mind. PHILIPPIANS 2:2 NIV

Special Events

The first fall of snow is not only an event but it is a magical event. You go to bed in one kind of world and wake up to find yourself in another quite different, and if this is not enchantment, then where is it to be found?   J. B. Priestley

The Best, Funniest, Most Challenging, Touching, Embarrassing, or Amazing Memories of this Christmas

Reflections from the season

Snow is falling outside my study window... I see nature once more playing endless variations in design and beauty.... In such simple yet eloquent ways, I am reminded that God is personal, revealing Himself continuously in the finite.

JUDITH C. LECHMAN

christmas celebration

Year _____

It is Christmas in the heart
that puts Christmas in the air.

W. T. ELLIS

Special Guests

_____

_____

_____

_____

_____

_____

_____

Memorable Gatherings

_____

_____

_____

_____

_____

_____

_____

_____

_____

_____

LET IT SNOW!

No matter how we may dread the rush…when Christmas Day comes there is still the same warm feeling we had as children, the same warmth that enfolds our hearts and our homes. JOAN WINMILL BROWN

Christmas Eve Celebration

_____
_____
_____
_____
_____
_____
_____
_____
_____
_____

Christmas Day Celebration

_____
_____
_____
_____
_____
_____
_____
_____
_____
_____
_____
_____

christmas Dinner

_____

_____

_____

_____

_____

_____

_____

_____

christmas Traditions Observed

_____

_____

_____

_____

_____

_____

_____

_____

Thoughtful Gestures & Cherished Gifts

_____

_____

_____

_____

_____

_____

_____

_____

_____

_____

_____

_____

_____

_____

It is in loving— not in being loved the heart is blest;
It is in giving—not in seeking gifts we find our quest.

christmas Greeting Sent

[Adhere
Christmas card or
newsletter here]

Holiday Photo

[Adhere Photo]

Be full of joy in the Lord always. I will say again, be full of joy. PHILIPPIANS 4:4 NCV

Special Events

_____

_____

_____

_____

_____

_____

_____

_____

_____

_____

_____

_____

_____

_____

_____

_____

_____

_____

Begin doing what you want to do now. We are not living in eternity.
We have only this moment, sparkling like a star in our hand—and melting like a snowflake.

The Best, Funniest, Most challenging, Touching, Embarrassing, or Amazing Memories of this christmas

Reflections from the season

For somehow, not only at Christmas, but all the long year through, the joy that you give to others is the joy that comes back to you.

JOHN GREENLEAF WHITTIER

christmas celebration

Year _____

What if Christmas, he thought,
doesn't come from a store.
What if Christmas, perhaps,
means a little bit more.

DR. SEUSS

Special Guests

_____
_____
_____
_____
_____
_____
_____

Memorable Gatherings

_____
_____
_____
_____
_____
_____

LET IT SNOW!

Christmas Eve was a night of song that wrapped itself about you like a shawl.
But it warmed more than your body. It warmed your heart . . .
filled it, too, with a melody that would last forever.   BESS STREETER ALDRICH

Christmas Eve Celebration

_____
_____
_____
_____
_____
_____
_____
_____

Christmas Day Celebration

_____
_____
_____
_____
_____
_____
_____
_____
_____

christmas Dinner

_____

_____

_____

_____

_____

_____

christmas Traditions Observed

_____

_____

_____

_____

_____

_____

_____

Thoughtful Gestures & Cherished Gifts

_____

_____

_____

_____

_____

_____

_____

_____

_____

_____

_____

_____

_____

_____

_____

_____

I love the Christmas-tide, and yet I notice this, each year I live;
I always like the gifts I get, But how I love the gifts I give!   CAROLYN WELLS

christmas Greeting Sent

[
Adhere
Christmas card or
newsletter here
 ]

Holiday Photo

[Adhere Photo]

My first copies of *Treasure Island* and *Huckleberry Finn* still have some
blue-spruce needles scattered in the pages. They smell of Christmas still. CHARLTON HESTON

Special Events

The shepherds returned, glorifying and praising God for all the things
they had heard and seen, which were just as they had been told.   LUKE 2:20 NIV

The Best, Funniest, Most challenging, Touching, Embarrassing, or Amazing Memories of this christmas

_____

_____

_____

_____

_____

_____

_____

_____

_____

_____

_____

_____

_____

_____

_____

Reflections from the season

Behind every joyful Christmas season are
busy hands and loving hands that make the memories
and then pack it all up for next year when once
again they'll have the joy of unpacking
the memories again.

SANDY LYNAM

christmas celebration

Year _____

 When I think of Christmas Eves, Christmas feasts, Christmas songs...I know it was not a short and transient gladness. It was—and is— a joy unspeakable and full of glory.

CORRIE TEN BOOM

Special Guests

_____

_____

_____

_____

_____

_____

_____

Memorable Gatherings

_____

_____

_____

_____

_____

_____

_____

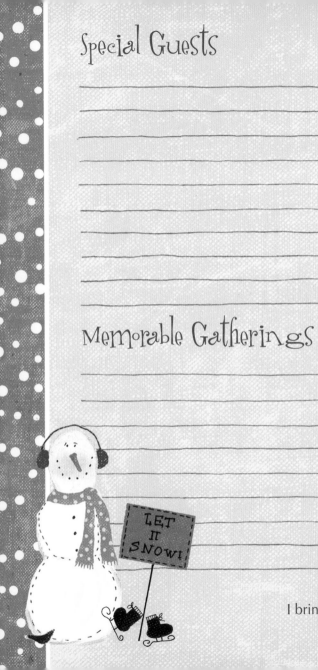

LET IT SNOW!

The angel said to them, "Do not be afraid; for behold,
I bring you good news of great joy which will be for all the people." LUKE 2:10 NASB

Christmas Eve Celebration

_____
_____
_____
_____
_____
_____
_____
_____
_____

Christmas Day Celebration

_____
_____
_____
_____
_____
_____
_____
_____
_____
_____

christmas Dinner

_____

_____

_____

_____

_____

_____

_____

_____

christmas Traditions Observed

_____

_____

_____

_____

_____

_____

_____

_____

_____

Thoughtful Gestures & Cherished Gifts

_____

_____

_____

_____

_____

_____

_____

_____

_____

_____

_____

_____

_____

_____

_____

_____

_____

O come, all ye faithful, Joyful and triumphant,
O come, ye, O come ye to Bethlehem! JOHN FRANCIS WADE

christmas Greeting sent

[Adhere
Christmas card or
newsletter here]

Holiday Photo

[Adhere Photo]

Beloved, let us love one another, for love is of God;
and everyone who loves is born of God and knows God.   1 JOHN 4:7 NKJV

Special Events

The ornaments upon our tree have secrets of their own,
of other trees and Christmases that each of them have known.   Kay Andrew

The Best, Funniest, Most challenging, Touching, Embarrassing, or Amazing Memories of this christmas

_____

_____

_____

_____

_____

_____

_____

_____

_____

_____

_____

_____

_____

_____

_____

_____

_____

Reflections from the season

Passing on joy is something which is very natural. We have no reason for not being joyful, since Christ is with us.

MOTHER TERESA

christmas celebration

Year _____

Heap on more wood!—the wind is chill;
but let it whistle as it will, we'll keep our
Christmas merry still.

SIR WALTER SCOTT

Special Guests

_____
_____
_____
_____
_____
_____
_____

Memorable Gatherings

_____
_____
_____
_____
_____
_____
_____

LET IT SNOW!

My brothers and sisters, be full of joy in the Lord.   PHILIPPIANS 3:1 NCV

christmas Eve Celebration

_____
_____
_____
_____
_____
_____
_____
_____

christmas Day Celebration

_____
_____
_____
_____
_____
_____
_____
_____
_____
_____
_____
_____

Christmas Dinner

_____

_____

_____

_____

_____

_____

Christmas Traditions Observed

_____

_____

_____

_____

_____

_____

_____

Thoughtful Gestures & Cherished Gifts

_____

_____

_____

_____

_____

_____

_____

_____

_____

_____

_____

_____

_____

_____

_____

_____

Gifts of time and love are surely the basic ingredients of a truly merry Christmas. PEG BRACKEN

christmas Greeting sent

[Adhere
Christmas card or
newsletter here]

Holiday Photo

[Adhere Photo   ]

Always be joyful. 1 THESSALONIANS 5:16 NLT

Special Events

_____

_____

_____

_____

_____

_____

_____

_____

_____

_____

_____

_____

_____

_____

Joyfulness keeps the heart and face young. A good laugh makes us better
friends with ourselves and everybody around us. ORISON SWETT MARDEN

The Best, Funniest, Most challenging, Touching, Embarrassing, or Amazing Memories of this christmas

_____
_____
_____
_____
_____
_____
_____
_____
_____
_____
_____
_____
_____
_____
_____
_____
_____
_____

Reflections from the Season

At Christmas play and
make good cheer, for Christmas
comes but once a year.

THOMAS TUSSER

christmas Celebration

Year _____

To act lovingly is to begin to feel
loving, and certainly to act joyfully
brings joy to others, which in turn
makes one feel joyful.

DOROTHY DAY

Special Guests

_____

_____

_____

_____

_____

_____

Memorable Gatherings

_____

_____

_____

_____

_____

_____

LET IT SNOW!

God decided in advance to adopt us into his own family....
This is what he wanted to do, and it gave him great pleasure. EPHESIANS 1:5 NLT

christmas Eve celebration

_____
_____
_____
_____
_____
_____
_____
_____

christmas Day celebration

_____
_____
_____
_____
_____
_____
_____
_____
_____

christmas Dinner

_____
_____
_____
_____
_____
_____
_____

christmas Traditions Observed

_____
_____
_____
_____
_____
_____
_____
_____

Thoughtful Gestures & Cherished Gifts

God must have said, "I know what I'll do, I'll send my LOVE right down there where they are. And I'll send it as a tiny baby, so they'll have to touch it, and they'll have to hold it close." GLORIA GAITHER

christmas Greeting sent

[Adhere
Christmas card or
newsletter here]

Holiday Photo

[Adhere Photo]

They ate together in their homes, happy to share their food with joyful hearts. ACTS 2:46 NCV

Special Events

_____

_____

_____

_____

_____

_____

_____

_____

_____

_____

_____

_____

_____

_____

_____

_____

Good humor and laughter are far too wonderful not to
come straight from the heart of God. BETH MOORE

The Best, Funniest, Most challenging, Touching, Embarrassing, or Amazing Memories of this christmas

_____
_____
_____
_____
_____
_____
_____
_____
_____
_____
_____
_____
_____
_____
_____
_____
_____

Reflections from the season